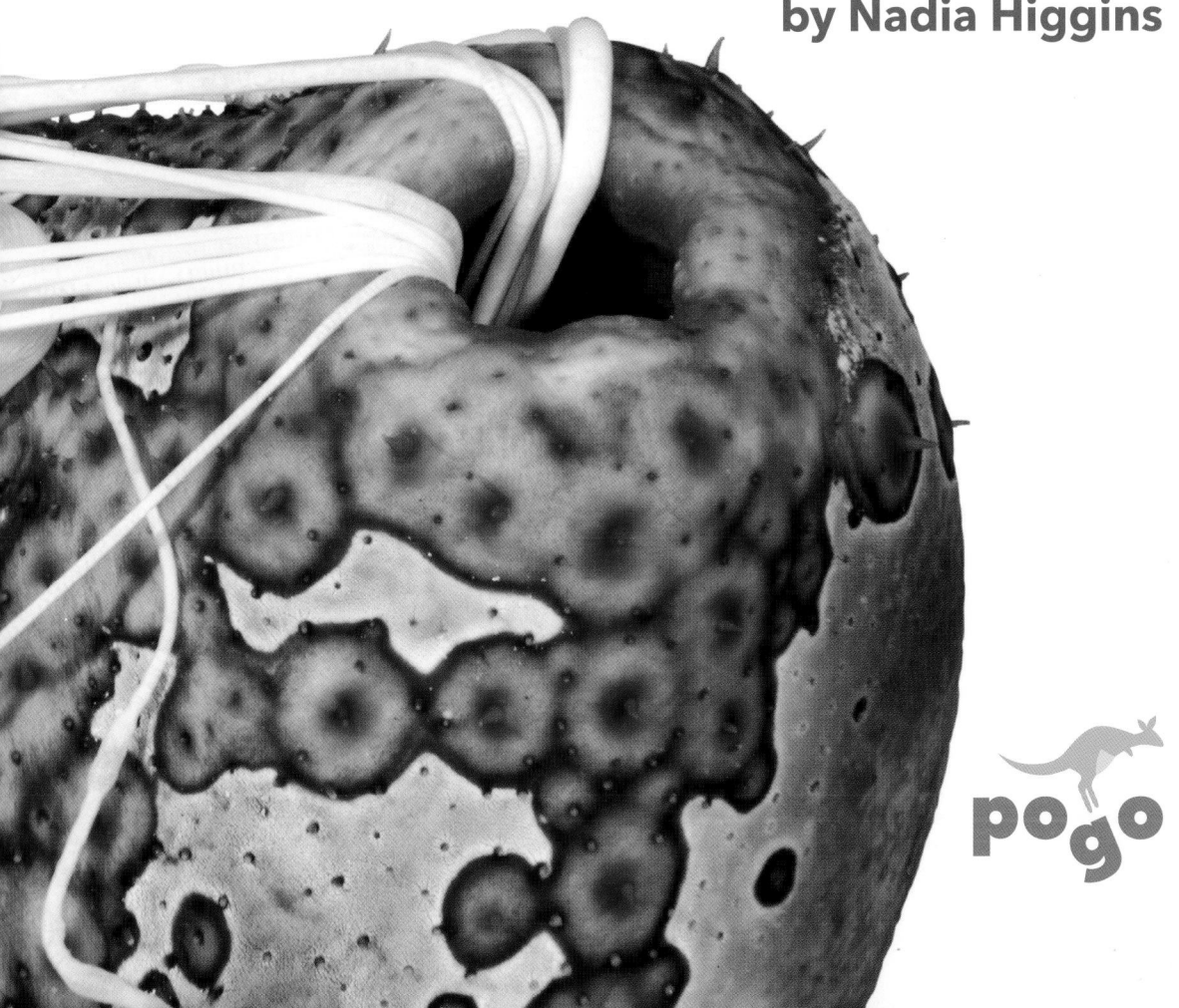

BACK OFF! ANIMAL DEFENSES
SLIMY ANIMALS

by Nadia Higgins

pogo

Ideas for Parents and Teachers

Pogo Books let children practice reading informational text while introducing them to nonfiction features such as headings, labels, sidebars, maps, and diagrams, as well as a table of contents, glossary, and index.

Carefully leveled text with a strong photo match offers early fluent readers the support they need to succeed.

Before Reading

• "Walk" through the book and point out the various nonfiction features. Ask the student what purpose each feature serves.

• Look at the glossary together. Read and discuss the words.

Read the Book

• Have the child read the book independently.

• Invite him or her to list questions that arise from reading.

After Reading

• Discuss the child's questions. Talk about how he or she might find answers to those questions.

• Prompt the child to think more. Ask: Have you seen any of the slimy animals mentioned in the book? Can you think of any slimy animals that aren't discussed?

Pogo Books are published by Jump!
5357 Penn Avenue South
Minneapolis, MN 55419
www.jumplibrary.com

Library of Congress Cataloging-in-Publication Data

Higgins, Nadia, author.
  Slimy animals / by Nadia Higgins.
    pages cm. – (Back off! Animal defenses)
  Audience: Ages 7-10.
  Summary: "Carefully leveled text and vibrant photographs introduce readers to slimy animals such as the hagfish, fulmar, tomato frog, and ribbon worm, and explore how they use slime to defend themselves against predators. Includes activity, glossary, and index."–Provided by publisher.
  Includes index.
  ISBN 978-1-62031-306-0 (hardcover: alk. paper) –
  ISBN 978-1-62496-372-8 (ebook)
  1. Animal chemical defenses–Juvenile literature.
  2. Animal defenses–Juvenile literature.
  3. Adaptation (Biology)–Juvenile literature. I. Title.
  QL759.H4455 2016
  591.47–dc23
                                          2015032608

Series Editor: Jenny Fretland VanVoorst
Series Designer: Anna Peterson
Book Designer: Ellen Schofield
Photo Researcher: Jenny Fretland VanVoorst

Photo Credits: Alamy, 4, 18-19, 23; Corbis, 12, 13; Getty, 6-7; Nature Picture Library, 8-9; Shutterstock, cover, 5, 14-15; SuperStock, 1, 10-11, 20-21; Thinkstock, 3, 16, 17.

Printed in the United States of America at Corporate Graphics in North Mankato, Minnesota.

TABLE OF CONTENTS

CHAPTER 1

SLIMED!

A hagfish slithers over the ocean floor. To a shark, the soft animal looks like easy **prey**. Snap! The shark attacks.

But the hagfish has a surprise. Slime gushes from its skin. The goo clogs the shark's snout and **gills**. The shark begins to choke. While it thrashes in terror, the hagfish swims away.

The hagfish wipes itself down after a slime attack. It ties itself in a knot. Then it slips the knot up and down its body.

TAKE A LOOK!

A ribbon worm lives in mud under the ocean. How does slime help it slip away from predators?

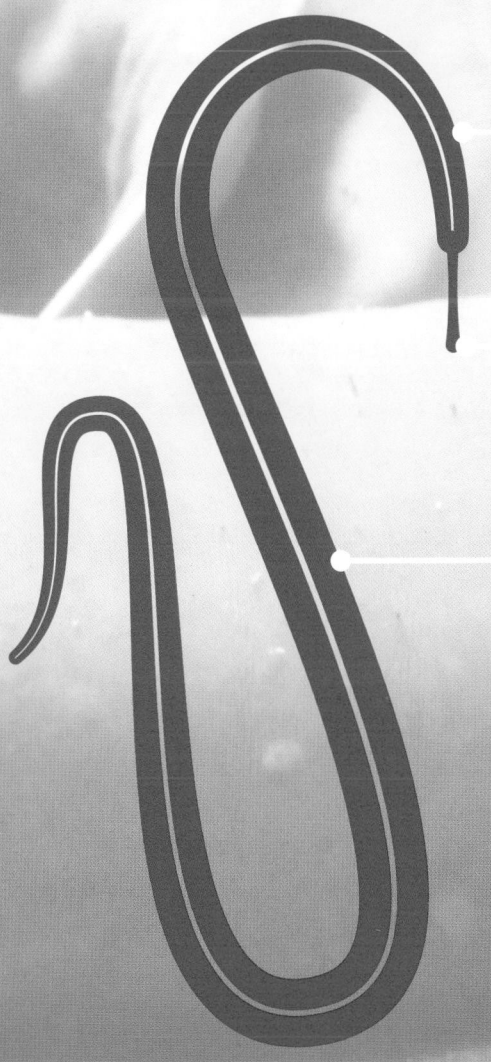

The skin makes a constant supply of slime.

This part is like a tongue. The worm attaches it to a surface.

Zip! It pulls its slippery body forward. Slime protects its skin from rough sand and rocks.

High on a cliff, a **fulmar** chick looks so helpless. But watch out! When a hungry **skua** comes too close, the baby opens its mouth. It blasts the big bird with **vomit**.

The skua had better fly away fast. The oily vomit can ruin its feathers. That could keep the bird from ever flying again.

DID YOU KNOW?

It's OK if some vomit gets on a fulmar. It has special feathers. The slime easily comes off.

A tomato frog's color warns its enemies. It says, "Don't eat me. Or else!"

When danger comes, the frog's skin oozes sticky slime. It looks just like school glue. The white stuff can gum up a **predator's** eyes and mouth. Its sticky power lasts for days.

CHAPTER 2
SLIMY TRICKS

In the deep ocean, a shrimp senses trouble. It can feel a fish coming closer. But the small creature does not swim away.

The shrimp opens its mouth. Glurp! Out comes a cloud of slime. It glows in the black water.

The light blinds the fish. Quickly, the shrimp scurries into the darkness.

adult cereal leaf beetle

In a wheat field, a cereal leaf beetle hatches. The little **larva** is yellow. Any hungry bird can see it.

Luckily, this baby bug has slime on its side. It covers its back with poop. A layer of jelly keeps the poop on. The bug is not so easy to spot now.

CHAPTER 3

BLOOD AND GUTS

It is noon in a Texas desert. A horned lizard squares off against a hungry coyote. The spiky lizard gets ready to shoot.

It closes its eyes. Squirt! Blood streams out of one eye. It sprays the coyote's mouth. The coyote chokes and spits, and the lucky lizard darts away.

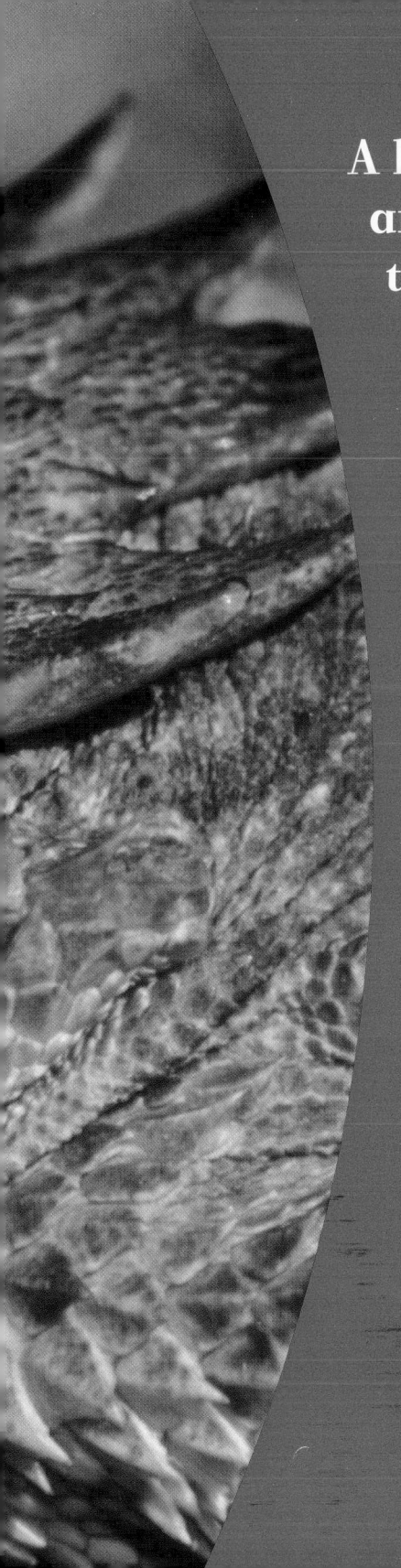

A horned lizard will shoot again
and again. It can squirt out half
the blood in its body.

A sea cucumber looks like a squishy lump. How could it possibly fight?

When danger comes, this animal squeezes special **muscles**. It shoots some guts out of its rear end. The guts have long, sticky threads. A hungry fish backs off. It does not want to get tangled up!

DID YOU KNOW?

The sea cucumber's guts drift away in the water. That's OK. The missing parts will grow back.

ACTIVITIES & TOOLS

MAKE YOUR OWN SLIME

Mix up a batch of slimy goo right in your own kitchen.

You will need:
- water
- borax
- white liquid glue
- food coloring
- measuring cup
- two bowls
- a spoon for stirring

Steps:

❶ Pour one cup of warm water into one of the bowls. Add one teaspoon of borax. Stir until you can't see grains of borax anymore.

❷ In the other bowl, combine ½ cup (.2 liters) of glue and ½ cup (.2 l) of water. Add a few drops of food coloring. Stir.

❸ Pour the glue mixture into the watery mixture. Keep stirring as a clump of slime starts to form.

❹ Pull out your slime. Stretch and roll the slime in your hands. The more you play with it, the stiffer it will get.

❺ Store your slime in a sealed plastic bag in your fridge.

Invent an animal to go with your slime. What is it called? Where does it live? How does it use its slime to keep safe? Draw a picture of your creation.

fulmar: A seabird that lives along the coast in England and France.

gills: The slits on a fish's body that let it take in oxygen from the water. Gills let fish live underwater without ever coming up for air.

larva: A baby insect. A larva looks very different from its parents.

muscle: A body part that makes animals move.

predator: An animal that kills other animals for food.

prey: An animal that is killed and eaten by other animals.

skua: A seabird that nests in the Arctic but has been observed as far south as Antarctica.

vomit: Throw up.

INDEX

TO LEARN MORE

Learning more is as easy as 1, 2, 3.

1) Go to www.factsurfer.com

2) Enter "slimyanimals" into the search box.

3) Click the "Surf" button to see a list of websites.

With factsurfer, finding more information is just a click away.